Python Programming for Beginners

A guide to Python computer language, computer programming, and learning Python fast!

Table Of Contents

Introduction

I want to thank you and congratulate you for downloading the book, "Python Programming for Beginners".

This book contains helpful information about Python computer language, what it is, and the different things it can be used for. This book is aimed at beginners to Python, and will take you through all the necessary steps to gain a good understanding of its parameters, and syntax.

At the completion of this guide, you will have a basic understanding of Python, how it works, and how to use it to create your very own program!

This book includes great tips and techniques that will help you to learn how to use the Python language to program! You will discover how to write commands in Python, and do functions such as solve mathematical equations with ease!

You will discover the skills needed to efficiently use the Python programming language, and use Python to create many different programs.

Thanks again for downloading this book, I hope you enjoy it!

Chapter 1:
Programming 101

Before you begin studying the Python programming language, you need to become familiar with computer programming or program development. This chapter will briefly initiate you in the programming world. And all that you will learn here will be useful once you try learning other programming languages.

Computers and Circuitries

Computer programming is not that different to creating electrical circuits. It can be safely said that an electrical circuit is a primitive form of a 'program'. For example, a simple light bulb circuit with an on and off switch is a program. You flip the switch; the light bulb lights up. On the other hand, a program is just like that. You open the program; it runs.

A computer is comprised of multiple circuitries. Using the analogy before, you can say that a computer is comprised of multiple programs by itself. Those little programs are embedded in the computer's hardware.

If that is the case, what is the purpose of programming? Why not just build a computer with programs in its hardware? Well, first of all, that is not a simple task. If you were to create a circuit board that has a Windows operating system built in, then you are going to have a big bulky computer in your room — not to mention that it will be expensive. The world's first general-purpose computer, ENIAC, took 680 – 1,800 square feet of space, and even with its immense size, it could only perform a few programs.

Also, just imagine the size of a calculator. Then, understand that Windows' calculator program is just around 1MB big. A game in a Nintendo cartridge can be as big as 32KB or more. If you were to create a program as large as 10MB, just imagine how many circuits you would need to create. In the case of Windows 7, it takes up 16GB...

Hardcoding programs in circuitries proved to be inefficient. Due to that, computers were designed to take advantage of digital instructions, programs, or software instead. Computers became machines programmed to translate and perform software.

After all, it is much faster to type in instructions in a programming language than creating a circuit blueprint and soldering some electrical components together.

Software and Programs

Programs are sets of instructions your computer reads and executes. To create common programs, you need to type your source code and compile it. On the other hand, in games, complex applications, and even web-based software, you might need to include some resources like audio, images, videos, etc.

As a new programmer, you will be sticking mostly to writing source code. You do not need to think about resources and what not. And to be honest, it might take some time before you get to include resources in your programs in Python.

Programming Language

A computer's main purpose is to follow the programs installed onto it. However, you cannot just write something like, "put this text on the screen", and expect your computer to do it.

Computers cannot comprehend human language. Even if you can give commands to people with utmost precision, your computer will not be able to follow your instructions. For computers to do your bidding or execute your program, you will need to write it using languages that they can understand — which are programming languages.

Chapter 2:
Python — A Programming Language

Many professional programmers say that Python is one of the easiest programming languages to learn. Unlike other programming languages, you do not need to remember a lot of complicated stuff in Python.

But what exactly is a programming language anyway? As mentioned before, you need to create a program using programming languages. As a language, Python has its own words and grammar rules. The rules and words it has do not differ much with the rules and words of other programming languages. It even shares some terms with the English language.

For example, if you want your program to display a message like, "Hello World," you need to type and execute this line on Python:

print ("Hello World")

That is how simple programming languages are. If you were to instruct your computer using the English language, you might have said this instead.

Print the sentence "Hello World" on the screen.

If you compare the two, it seems that when using programming language to give instructions to the computer, you need to speak robotically. In programming language, one statement or one line of command only requires a verb (action or command) and an object (receiver of the action or object of the action). Sometimes, all you need to type is a single command keyword.

It might sound simple, but there are some quirky parts that you must know. Just like human language, programming languages also follow grammar rules or syntax. Unfortunately, syntax rules of programming languages are strict. If you make a mistake, expect that the computer will not be able to follow your instruction. It might return an error or even crash if it tries to read and execute a line with incorrect syntax.

For example, if you reverse the position of the elements of the print statement mentioned a while ago, this would happen:

>>> ("Hello World") print

File "<stdin>", line 1

  ("Hello World") print

SyntaxError: invalid syntax

>>>

Python's syntax rules will be discussed later. For now, it is time for you to prepare the things that you need.

Prep Yourself

Thanks to the previous chapter, you may now have a decent idea about what computer programming is and how everything relates to each other. Now, for programming you are required to have a basic knowledge about logic, abstract algebra, and college algebra.

In programming, you need to compare values most of the time, and occasionally, you might need to do it arithmetically and/or logically. Alternatively, you must have some basic knowledge about sets.

On the other hand, you must make sure that your program's flow is logical and will always lead to the result that you want. If ever there is an undesirable result, you must have a presence of mind and plan how to prevent that from happening, or devise a process for how your program will handle it.

Do not worry about those things too much. Even if you do not have those traits or knowledge yet, you can always learn them. Also, if you are passionate about programming, you will learn to develop these traits as you study and create programs.

Your Tools and Wares

Once you're prepared for programming, what is next? You need to prepare your 'programming kit'. Of course, the number one requirement for programming is a computer. Ideally, a typical computer running on Microsoft Windows is enough for your programming needs.

Computer

Take note that you do not need a high-end computer for programming, especially if you are just starting. Most of the programs that you will develop will probably be limited to using small chunks of resources of your computer or device.

Truth be told, it is an advantage to use 'weak' computers for programming. Using a slow computer will make you warier about the performance of your program. If ever your program has some inefficient codes in it, you will immediately feel the performance degradation it will cause. And that will lead to immediate awareness of your inefficient coding of your program.

Operating System

When it comes to operating systems, it is not necessary to use Microsoft Windows. Python code will work on almost any operating system environment. If you have a computer running on Mac OS or a Linux distro, then use it.

Python

Of course, you will need Python. As of this writing, the latest version of Python is Python 3.4.3. To get Python, you must go to https://www.python.org/downloads/.

In the download page, you have two primary choices of Python versions. The first one is 3.4.3, which is the stable release. And the second one is 2.7.9, which is the stable legacy version of Python.

What is the difference between the two? Well, Python version 2.7.9 is the older, more stable release of Python. Python has reached tremendous popularity with its versions 2.x.x. And due to that, most Python programmers have developed their programs under this version. As of now, most of the examples and programs made with Python use Python version 2.x.x.

Unfortunately, Python version 2.x.x is not perfect. It has its own problems. And it is said that fixing those problems and incompatibilities will require a lot of work. In addition, adding functionalities has become a problem, too. Because of these reasons, Python version 3.x.x was born.

Python 3.x.x experienced major changes when it comes to syntax and performance. Unluckily, it is not that backwards compatible with programs or source code made using Python 2.x.x. Nevertheless, it is possible to port those source codes in Python 3.x.x. You might need to use a third party program.

Alternatively, you might just need to rewrite the source code from scratch. And of course, you cannot fully use source code made in Python 3.x.x with Python 2.x.x.

That is just a summary of the things you need to know about the two versions. In this book, you will be taught of Python version 3.x.x.

Anyway, aside from the two versions on the page, you will see other links for other version releases of Python. If you see any version higher than the stable release, it is probable that it is still a beta release and it might contain some bugs.

Installing Python

After downloading, you can simply open the installer package and let it run. An installation window will pop up and all you need to do is to follow the steps that are indicated on the installation program.

But hold on and do not just click your way out of the installation. You will need to take note of the installation path of Python. You will need it later.

On the other hand, if you are using Linux, it is possible that your Linux distro came with Python preinstalled. However, it is possible that the Python version it has is version 2.x.x. You can check the version of Python you have in your package manager or using the terminal. On the terminal, just type:

$ python --version

To get the latest version of Python, make sure that you are connected to the internet. After that, you can download and install Python using your Linux' package manager or terminal.

If you are going to use the package manager, you can just use the search function and download Python. In case that you want to use the terminal, make sure that you are logged in as root or a power user. On the other hand, you can just use sudo. For example:

$ sudo apt-get install python3.4

Source Code Editor

In order to create a program, you need to type your source code. Unfortunately, Python does not come with a source code editor. However, it does have an interactive mode or interpreter mode. Python's interpreter mode will be discussed later.

If you are on Microsoft Windows, you can just use Notepad. On the other hand, Linux distros usually have preinstalled source code editors. If you do not like the one that is in your Linux, you can try other source code editors such as Emacs, Vim, or Ed.

By the way, Notepad is not really a source code editor. It lacks the necessary features, such as syntax highlighting, for it to aid you in writing your source code. Due to that, it is advisable that you get Notepad++. Notepad++ is a free source code editor that you can use instead of the simple text editor Notepad.

Once you're ready, proceed onto the next chapter to begin exploring Python.

Chapter 3:
Programming and Interactive Mode of Python

Python offers two ways to create programs. The first one is programming and the second one is interactive mode.

As a beginner, you will be spending more time in interactive mode. And as you progress, you will slowly shift to programming mode. But what are the differences between the two?

Interactive Mode — Python Interpreter

The interactive mode or Python's interpreter is well suited for those people who are new to the programming language. Typically, most people think that they need to write and finish their source codes first before they can check if what they did is right.

However, to make the steep learning curve of programming more relaxed and easier, some programming languages like Python offer interactive modes. The interactive mode is a console like program wherein your statements or lines of codes will be executed almost immediately.

For example, if you want to learn how the print keyword works in Python, you do not need to go to your source code editor, write the print keyword, save the file, and run it in Python.

All you need to do is to open the Python interpreter, type the print keyword together with its required arguments, and press Enter. The interpreter will immediately give you a feedback on how the print keyword works.

In print's case, you will immediately see that the program will print or display the argument that you input together with print. The explanation might be confusing at first, but you do not need to absorb all of that just yet.

To get a more solid idea about Python's interpreter, try opening it up. If you are using windows, you can just open the start menu. Go to Programs > Python 3.4 > Python 3.4 (command line). Once you click that, a command console like window will appear.

If you are using Windows, you will see this text on the command line prompt:

Python 3.4.2 (v3.4.2:ab2c023a9432, Oct 6 2014) [MSC v.1600 32 bit (Intel)] on win32

Type "help", "copyright". "credits" or "license" for more information.

>>>

Note: The author is using Python 3.4.2 hence the Python 3.4.2 header.

In the interpreter, the three chevrons or three greater than signs (>>>) is your command prompt. When it is on the screen, it means that you can type in a statement and execute it using the enter key.

For example, you want to display the text "Hello World" in Python or your program. You will need to type:

print ("Hello World")

And press Enter. Once you do that, this will happen.

>>> print ("Hello World")

Hello World

>>>

The first line is the command or statement that you just typed. After you press the enter key, the interpreter will process the command and bring you the result. In the example, Python displayed the Hello World text immediately after the command. Then, since the processing of the previous statement was finished, the command prompt was displayed once again.

Programming Mode — .py File

That is how the simple the command line or Python's interactive mode is. When it comes to the programming mode, you need to open your source code editor, type the statement, and save the file as a .py file.

For example, type:

print ("Hello World")

Then save it as helloworld.py on your desktop. If you are on Windows, go to the file's location and open it. If Python was installed properly, you can open .py files as if they are already programs in your system. On the technical side of things, it means that .py files are already associated with the Python executable and every time you will open a .py file, the Python executable will run and process the code within the file — just like when you open Microsoft Word .doc or document files.

When you do run the file that you just created, a small window like the command console will appear in split seconds. You might think that the 'small program' you created did not work. However, it did.

Unfortunately, the program did not run for long enough for you to be able to spot the Hello World display. For you to be able to see it, you will need to put something to pause the program. But that will be discussed later. For now, you have an idea as to why you cannot experiment freely on the programming mode of Python, and should begin with the interactive mode.

Chapter 4:
Python Statements and Syntax

A program is a set of instructions used to accomplish a goal. In order to create one, you must write your source code using a programming language. How can you write one? Well, here are a few things you need to know.

Statements

Statements are the building blocks of your program. In programming, statements are more like commands or instructions. Every statement makes the computer do something for you. To make it simpler, a statement is a line of code in Python. Below is an example of a statement:

print ("Hello World")

In the example, you instruct the program or computer to display the text Hello World. A statement contains elements or internal components that you need to place in order for the computer to perform an instruction. In the example, you have used two elements. The first one is a keyword or command, which is print. The second one is an argument or parameter, which the keyword needs to receive in order for it to function.

In order for a statement to function well or to work, it must follow the programming language's syntax. In the previous chapter, it was emphasized that if you exchange the position of the argument and the keyword in the statement, Python will return an error.

Syntax

In programming language, you need to follow syntax. Syntax is the collection of rules you need to follow in order to create a correct statement in programming languages. Just like in English grammar, one small mistake in writing your sentence may change the context of what you are trying to say. Unfortunately, the rules in computer programming are much stricter. Nevertheless, it is much simpler and easier to remember.

White Space and Lines

Continuous spaces and tabs are generally ignored in Python. Even if you leave a blank line in Python, Python's parser will just ignore it and skip to the next line. You can try that in the interpreter. Just place some spaces and press the enter key. As you can see, Python will not do anything and will just display the command prompt again.

Even if you try putting a lot of spaces between a keyword and its argument, Python will not give you any error messages. For example:

>>> print   ("Hello World")

Hello World

>>>

New Line

In other programming languages, you need to place a semicolon to indicate that a statement has ended. In grammar, those semicolons are just like periods. In Python, you do not need to do that. All you need to do is to end the statement or a 'logical line' with a new line or by pressing the enter key.

Of course, in some cases, new lines do not terminate a statement. For example, by doing an explicit or implicit joining (or extending a statement over the new line), the new line will not terminate the statement.

Explicit Joining

As mentioned before, every line of code in Python is a statement. However, it does not mean that you have to stick with 'literally' putting a huge statement in one line. It can be daunting and it can be an eyesore to do. In order to work around that, you will need to cut the statement into multiple lines and join them together. For example:

print ("This is a long paragraph that you should cut into many lines in order to reduce the length of each line that it will create. It is important to be somewhat organized when programming")

That is one line. And if you are coding in a source code editor, it will exceed the width of the viewport, and you will need to scroll right to view the rest of that long statement. Due to that, you will need to cut that into parts, this is how you do it:

*print ("This a long paragraph that you should cut *

*into many lines in order to reduce the length of *

*each line that it will create. It is important *

to be somehow organized when programming")

If you try that in the interpreter, the command prompt of the interpreter will change to an ellipsis (…). For example:

*>>> print ("This a long paragraph that you should cut *

*… into many lines in order to reduce the length of *

*… each line that it will create. It is important *

… to be somehow organized when programming")

This a long paragraph that you should cut into many lines in order to reduce the length of each line that it will create. It is important to be somehow organized when programming

>>>

Implicit Joining

Aside from using a backslash in order to perform explicit joining, there are some ways to join a statement with multiple 'physical lines'. As of now, you do not need to learn it, but here is an example:

name_of_days = ['Monday', 'Tuesday',

'Wednesday', 'Thursday', 'Friday',

'Saturday', 'Sunday']

Since the code is giving out a set of values and the line is not yet closed since the programmer has not provided the closing square bracket (]), Python has allowed to let the programmer use the next line and combine it to the statement. Below is another example:

>>> print ("Hello World",

... "And Welcome!")

Hello World And Welcome!

>>>

Indentation

Placing a space or a tab before a statement will make Python think that you have place an indentation. Indentations in Python will make the interpreter think that you are creating a code block in your program. In the interpreter, you cannot just place an indentation without proper reason. For example:

>>>   print ("Hello World")

    File "<stdin>", line 1

        print ("Hello World")

IndentationError: unexpected indent

>>>

You will learn about indentation later. Just make sure that you do not put any spaces before the statement, and you will be good to go.

Letter Casing

Take note that Python is picky when it comes to the casing of the keywords you use among other things. Fortunately, most of the keywords should be in all lowercase. Adding a capital letter at the start, in the middle, or placing all letters in the keyword in all caps will make you receive an error from Python. For example:

>>> PRINT ("Hello World")

Traceback (most recent call last):

   File "<stdin>", line 1, in <module>

NameError: name 'PRINT' is not defined

>>> Print ("Hello World")

Traceback (most recent call last):

   File "<stdin>", line 1, in <module>

NameError: name 'Print' is not defined

>>>

Chapter 5:
Variables, Data, Operators, and Expressions

As mentioned a while ago, statements need to contain some core elements before they can give out a proper instruction to the computer or interpreter. Aside from keywords, statements can also contain variables, data, operators, and expressions.

Variables, data, operators, and expressions are the little things that will make your program work. Mostly, you will be working with them.

Data

Data are numbers and strings (text) in your program. They are the ones that you need to manipulate in order for your program to do your bidding. To manipulate them, you can use operators. And to store them, you need variables.

Numbers

In Python, you can use positive and negative numbers. You can also use them in decimal, octal, or hexadecimal form. If ever you need to put an octal number, just place a 0 before the octal number. If you need to put a hexadecimal number, just place 0x before the number. For example:

>>> *print (255)*

255

>>> *print (off)*

Variables

Variables are containers for your data. They are there to 'remember' or store the data you need. You can always change them at any time. On the other hand, for those who have experienced programming in other languages, you might ask if you can create constants in Python. Constants are variables with unchangeable values — just like in Math.

If you do need to create a constant in Python, just assign a value in a variable and do not change it. However, it does not mean that there are no constants in Python. Python has built-in constants such as False, which has a value of False, and True, which has a value of True.

Variables can be made by creating an identifier. An identifier is a name for your variable. You can use the letter x, y, or z. You can use words such as thisIsaVariable or variablex. There are rules in creating the right identifier and they are:

- Identifiers must only have numbers, letters, or underscores, but a letter or an underscore must accompany a number

- Identifiers can contain one or more characters

- Identifiers must not start with a number

- Identifiers must not be the same with keywords, commands, or built-in constants in Python

- Identifiers are case sensitive; the variable named x is different from the variable named X

To create a variable, you must assign a value to it. For example:

>>> x = 123

>>>

You can check if a variable exists or check a variable's data by just typing it in the interpreter. For example:

>>> x

123

>>>

If you have not created a variable first and you try to check or call it, you will receive an error. For example:

>>> y

Traceback (most recent call last):

> *File "<stdin>", line 1, in <module>*

NameError: name 'y' is not defined

You can use variables directly to commands or keywords that are in need of values. For example:

>>> x = "Hello World"

>>> print (x)

Hello World

>>>

Operators

Operators are signs and symbols that you can use to manipulate data and variables. One of the operators that you have seen so far is the assignment operator, which has the symbol (=). There are multiple operator types in Python. For now, you will be introduced to the basic ones, which are arithmetic operators.

Arithmetic Operators

Arithmetic operators are not different from Math operators. Arithmetic operators in Python are + (addition), - (subtraction), * (multiplication), and / (division).

Expressions

Expressions are the combination of data, variables, and operators. Expressions are statements that can be evaluated and can return a result. You can assign expressions to variables. For example:

>>> a = 1 + 2

In this case, the variable a will not store the expression 1 + 2, but instead, Python will evaluate the expression then assign the result to the variable. So, if you check the value of variable a, then this will happen:

>>> a

3

>>>

On the other hand, you can use variables in your expressions and assign them to another variable. For example:

>>> b = 2

>>> c = 65

>>> d = b * c

>>> d

130

>>>

When assigning variables, take note that the expression will be evaluated first before the result gets assigned to the variable. Because of that, if you have a variable and assign an expression that contains the same variable, the variable will only receive the result after the expression is evaluated. For example:

>>> b = 10

>>> c = 99

>>> d = b − c

-89

>>>

Chapter 6:
Functions or Commands You Need for Basic Programs

Of course, you cannot just make a program with variables, operators, expressions, and data alone. You need some other functions to make your program have a 'purpose'. In this chapter, you will learn some functions or commands in Python that you can use to make your program become a 'program'.

print

You have seen this in the examples before. Print is a function that you can use to print numbers and strings on your programs. For example:

>>> print (123)

123

>>> print ("Print something")

Print something

>>> x = 2

>>> print (x)

2

>>>

Take note that in order for functions to work and for the argument you type to work, make sure that you enclose the arguments inside parentheses.

input

If you want your user to type in something in your program and you want to use the value or data that the user will submit, use the input function. Input can pause the program and wait for the user to type in something. For example:

>>> input()

—

The program will pause for a while, and will proceed after the user presses the enter key. On the other hand, you can provide a prompt for the user to read to know what to do. For example:

>>> input ("Press the enter key to exit this prompt...")

Press the enter key to exit this prompt..._

Also, you can directly assign the input of the user to a variable by doing this:

>>> x = input("Please enter a number: ")

Please enter a number: 2

>>> x

2

>>>

With those two alone, you can create a basic program such a calculator in Python. Below is an example of a calculator program using all the things you learned in the previous chapter:

print ("Welcome to the calculator program.")

print ("Note that this program can only add two numbers.")

print ("Note that you need to enter numbers only.")

print ("Putting letters in the input will crash this program.")

print ("The program is now starting.")

x = input ("Enter the first number you want to add: ")

y = input ("Enter the second number you want to add: ")

z = x + y

print ("The sum of the two numbers are:", z)

input ("The program is now over. Press enter to exit this program.")

Conclusion

Thank you again for downloading this book!

I hope this book was able to help you learn more about Python!

The next step is to put the strategies provided into use, and begin using Python!

Finally, if you enjoyed this book, please take the time to share your thoughts and post a review on Amazon. It'd be greatly appreciated!

Thank you and good luck!

www.ingramcontent.com/pod-product-compliance
Lightning Source LLC
Chambersburg PA
CBHW071554080326
40690CB00056B/2028